World Languages

Colors in French

Daniel Nunn

Chicago, Illinois

www.capstonepub.com
Visit our website to find out more information about Heinemann-Raintree books.

To order:
☎ Phone 800-747-4992
🖥 Visit www.capstonepub.com to browse our catalog and order online.

Edited by Rebecca Rissman, Dan Nunn, and Sian Smith
Designed by Joanna Hinton-Malivoire
Picture research by Elizabeth Alexander
Production by Alison Parsons
Originated by Capstone Global Library Ltd
Printed and bound in the United States of America in North Mankato, Minnesota. 112012   007034

16 15 14 13 12
10 9 8 7 6 5 4 3 2 1

Library of Congress Cataloging-in-Publication Data
Nunn, Daniel.
  Colors in French : les couleurs / Daniel Nunn.
    p. cm.—(World languages - Colors)
  Includes bibliographical references and index.
  ISBN 978-1-4329-6651-5—ISBN 978-1-4329-6658-4 (pbk.) 1. French language—Textbooks for foreign speakers—English—Juvenile literature. 2. Colors—Juvenile literature. I. Title.
  PC2129.E5N86 2013
  448.2'421—dc23   2011046542

Acknowledgments
We would like to thank Shutterstock for permission to reproduce photographs: pp.4 (© Phiseksit), 5 (© Stephen Aaron Rees), 6 (© Tischenko Irina), 7 (© Tony Magdaraog), 8 (© szefei), 9 (© Picsfive), 10 (© Eric Isselée), 11 (© Yasonya), 12 (© Nadezhda Bolotina), 13 (© Maryna Gviazdovska), 14 (© Erik Lam), 15 (© Eric Isselée), 16 (© Ruth Black), 17 (© blueskies9), 18 (© Alexander Dashewsky), 19 (© Michele Perbellini), 20 (© Eric Isselée), 21 (© Roman Rvachov).

Cover photographs reproduced with permission of Shutterstock: dog (© Erik Lam), strawberry (© Stephen Aaron Rees), fish (© Tischenko Irina). Back cover photograph of a parrot reproduced with permission of Shutterstock (© Eric Isselée).

We would like to thank Séverine Ribierre for her invaluable assistance in the preparation of this book.

Every effort has been made to contact copyright holders of material reproduced in this book. Any omissions will be rectified in subsequent printings if notice is given to the publisher.

Contents

Rouge

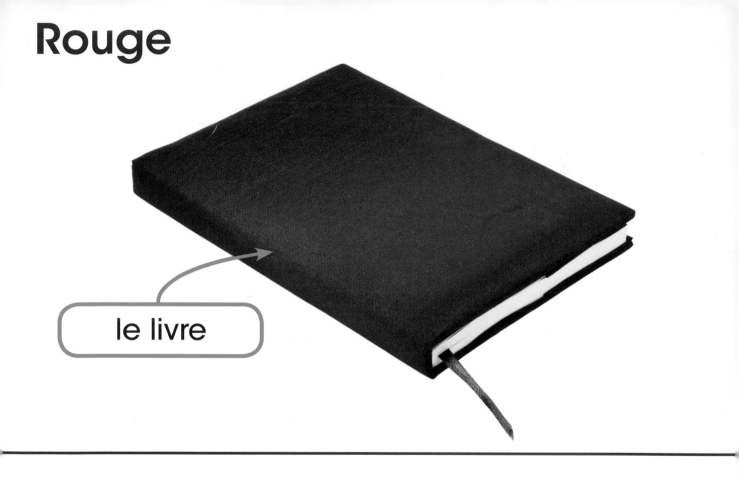

le livre

Le livre est rouge.

la fraise

La fraise est rouge.

Orange

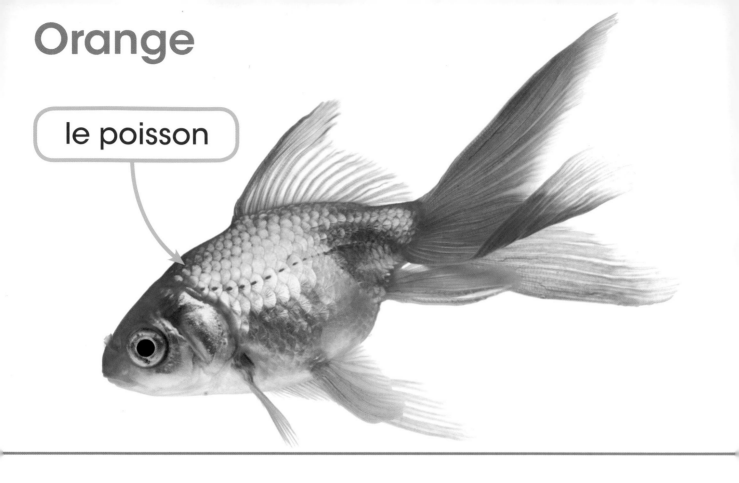

le poisson

Le poisson est orange.

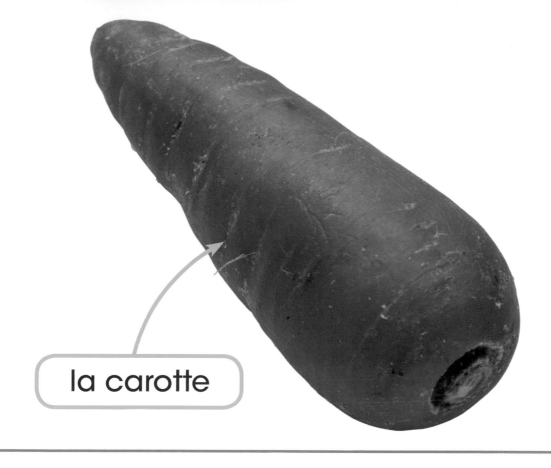

la carotte

La carotte est orange.

Jaune

la fleur

La fleur est jaune.

la banane

La banane est jaune.

Vert

l'oiseau

L'oiseau est vert.

la pomme

La pomme est verte.

Bleu

le T-shirt

Le T-shirt est bleu.

la tasse

La tasse est bleue.

Marron

le chien

Le chien est marron.

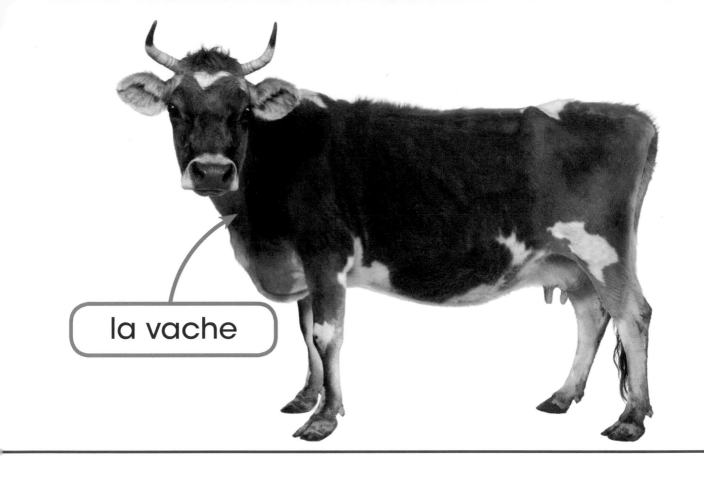

la vache

La vache est marron.

Rose

le gâteau

Le gâteau est rose.

le chapeau

Le chapeau est rose.

Blanc

le lait

Le lait est blanc.

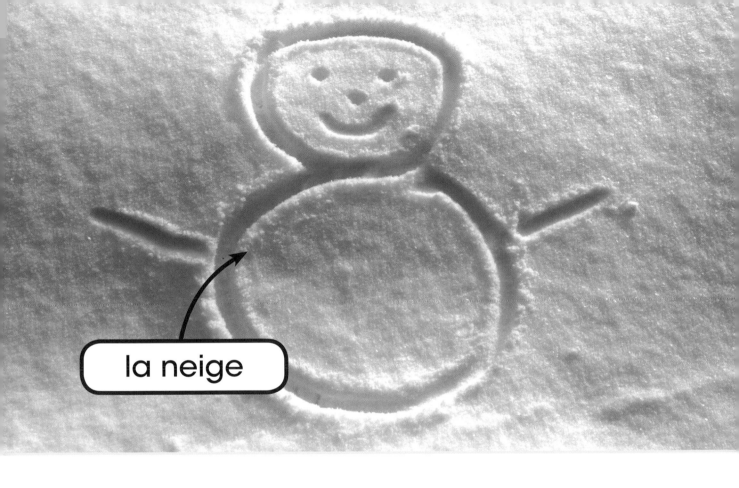

la neige

La neige est blanche.

Noir

le chat

Le chat est **noir**.

le parapluie

Le parapluie est **noir**.

Dictionary

French Word	How To Say It	English Word
banane	ba-nan	banana
blanc / blanche	blon / blonsh	white
bleu / bleue	bluh / bluh	blue
carotte	ka-rot	carrot
chapeau	shap-oh	hat
chat	cha	cat
chien	che-an	dog
est	ay	is
fleur	flur	flower
fraise	frayz	strawberry
gâteau	ga-tow	cake
jaune	jone	yellow
la	la	the
lait	lay	milk
le	luh	the
livre	leevre	book

French Word	How To Say It	English Word
marron	ma-ron	brown
neige	nehj	snow
noir	nwoir	black
oiseau	wa-zo	bird
orange	or-onj	orange
parapluie	pa-ra-plwee	umbrella
poisson	pwo-sohn	fish
pomme	pom	apple
rose	rohz	pink
rouge	rooj	red
T-shirt	tee-shirt	T-shirt
tasse	tas	cup
vache	vash	cow
vert / verte	vair / vairt	green

It has only been possible to provide a rough guide to pronunciations, which you can find in the "How To Say It" columns.

Index

Notes for Parents and Teachers

In French, nouns are either masculine or feminine. The word for "the" changes accordingly—either le (masculine) or la (feminine). Sometimes adjectives have different spellings too, depending on whether the noun is masculine or feminine. This is why some of the colors have more than one spelling.